Us~
Christmas
Quiz Book

Written, designed
and illustrated by
Santa's Little Helpers

1

(1) **Complete the lyrics: "Jingle bells, jingle bells, jingle..."**
   a) ...on the sleigh
   b) ...night and day
   c) ...all the way

(2) **Which part of a reindeer grows nearly 1 inch (2.5cm) a day?**
   a) tail   b) fur   c) antlers

(3) **What are the pointy leaves on a Christmas tree called?**
   a) spines
   b) needles
   c) spindles

(4) **Which movie is set at Christmas time?**
   a) *The Polar Express*
   b) *Ice Age*
   c) *Frozen*

(5) **Santa's hat is:**
   a) red and white
   b) red and green
   c) green and white

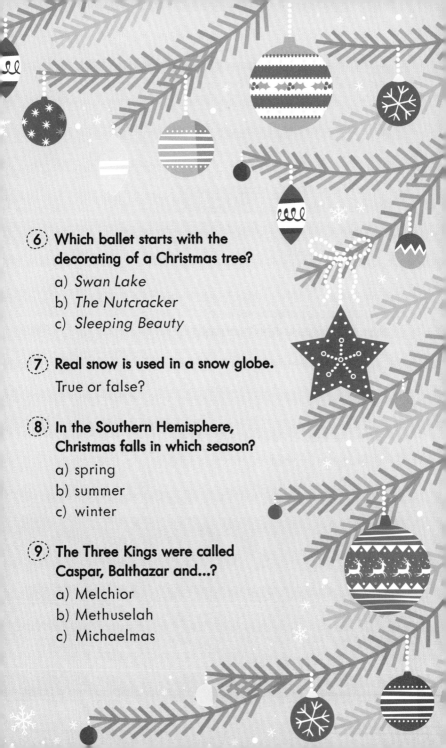

6 Which ballet starts with the decorating of a Christmas tree?

a) *Swan Lake*
b) *The Nutcracker*
c) *Sleeping Beauty*

7 Real snow is used in a snow globe. True or false?

8 In the Southern Hemisphere, Christmas falls in which season?

a) spring
b) summer
c) winter

9 The Three Kings were called Caspar, Balthazar and...?

a) Melchior
b) Methuselah
c) Michaelmas

1 Louis Tomlinson was born on Christmas Eve, 1991. Name the pop group that made him famous.

a) The Wanted
b) One Direction
c) Backstreet Boys

2 What is Scrooge's usual response to the words "Merry Christmas"?

a) "You're fired!"
b) "Nincompoopery!"
c) "Bah! Humbug!"

3 What type of creatures help Santa get ready for Christmas?

a) dwarfs
b) gnomes
c) elves

4 ...And where do they work?

a) Santa's School
b) Santa's Workshop
c) Santa's Hotel

5 **What is a snow storm called?**
  a) blizzard
  b) monsoon
  c) cyclone

6 **What's another name for the Three Kings?**
  a) prophets   b) magi   c) pharaohs

7 **What do you hang out on Christmas Eve?**
  a) a stocking
  b) a red hat
  c) a bell

8 **Which is NOT one of Santa's reindeer?**
  a) Ranger
  b) Dasher
  c) Blitzen

1 Traditionally, which bird is NOT roasted at Christmas?

a) goose   b) ostrich   c) turkey

2 What does Santa hope to find in your house on Christmas Eve?

a) everyone wide awake
b) a roaring fire in the fireplace
c) a snack for himself and his reindeer

3 What's the main ingredient in mince pies?

a) meat   b) fruit   c) cheese

4 More Christmas cards are sold each year than birthday cards.

True or false?

5 What are a snowman's eyes traditionally made from?

a) coal   b) coins   c) buttons

6 **What do people do under mistletoe?**
   a) dance   b) sing   c) kiss

7 **Which Christmas treat is red, white
and shaped like a shepherd's crook?**
   a) candy cane
   b) lollipop
   c) humbug

8 **You leave a carrot out for me on Christmas Eve.
I help pull Santa's sleigh,
and light the way on foggy nights.**
   Who am I?

9 **Name the furry green
meanie who wants
to cancel Christmas.**
   a) The Yutz
   b) The Grinch
   c) The Snitch

1 Which star could Santa use to navigate his way home?

a) the North Star
b) the Dog Star
c) Rigel

2 Mary rode to Bethlehem on a...

a) horse?
b) camel?
c) donkey?

3 What's the name of the place that's always winter but never Christmas?

a) Narnia   b) Neverland   c) The Black Isle

4 Roughly how many people were involved in the biggest ever snowball fight?

a) eight hundred
b) eight thousand
c) eight million

(5) **According to the song, what happened when "Santa got stuck up the chimney"?**

    a) he turned blue

    b) he had a sneezing fit

    c) he dropped his sack of toys

(6) **I grew up in a forest...**

    ...until someone came and chopped me down.
    They took me inside and dressed me in shiny tinsel.

    What am I?

(7) **Which is NOT a traditional way to count down the days to Christmas?**

    a) Advent candle

    b) Advent calendar

    c) Advent calculator

(8) **What's the most popular type of Christmas cake worldwide?**

    a) fruit cake

    b) chocolate cake

    c) cheesecake

1 What's the biggest number of Christmas cards ever sent by one person in a year?

a) 628   b) 6,282   c) 62,824

2 Who banned Christmas?

a) The Sheriff of Nottingham
b) Lord Protector Oliver Cromwell
c) Prime Minister Margaret Thatcher

3 Traditional Advent wreaths have four candles. What do the candles represent?

a) the four weeks of advent
b) North, South, East and West
c) the four horsemen of the apocalypse

4) In a Christmas ballet called *The Nutcracker,* what's the ruler of the land of sweets called?

a) Nutcracker Prince
b) Sugar Plum Fairy
c) Mother Ginger

5) Complete the title of the carol: *Little...*

a) donkey   b) doggy   c) horsey

6) Reindeer aren't deer.
True or false?

7) Which fruit is traditionally put in Christmas stockings?

a) strawberries   b) apples   c) oranges

Match each clue to the name
of one of Santa's reindeer.

1) Looks like a
star with a tail

2) Matchmaker
with a bow
and arrow

3) The youngest
and most famous of
Santa's reindeer

b) Donner

a) Dasher

c) Prancer

d) Comet

1 What's the name for the fruit bread that's eaten in Germany over Christmas?

a) battenberg   b) stollen   c) berliner

2 I'm a green-furred, Christmas-hating loner, and live in a cave on a cliff above Whoville. Who am I?

3 Which King of England was crowned on Christmas Day 1066?

a) William the Conqueror
b) Richard I
c) Henry VIII

4 Which is NOT another name for Santa Claus?

a) Father Christmas
b) Peter Quince
c) Kris Kringle

5 **What's odd about the title character in the movie *Elf*?**

a) he's not actually an elf

b) he's a walking, talking Christmas tree – an Evergreen Life Form

c) he doesn't believe in Santa Claus

6 **What day of the year is Boxing Day and St. Stephen's Day?**

a) December 26th

b) December 27th

c) December 28th

7 **Complete the song title: *Rudolph the...***

a) green-nosed reindeer

b) white-nosed reindeer

c) red-nosed reindeer

8 **A snowflake is lighter than a raindrop.**

True or false?

1 Why was Jesus born in a stable?

 a) the inn was too expensive

 b) the inn was too dangerous

 c) the inn was full

2 In North America, what sweet and creamy drink is popular around Christmastime?

 a) eggneg   b) eggnog   c) eggyegg

3 Every Christmas, a research station at the South Pole holds a two-mile race around the Pole. What's the race called?

 a) The Race around the World

 b) The Slide Around the Pole

 c) The Snowlympic Games

4 ...And what's the prize for winning the race?

 a) a five-minute hot shower

 b) a pet penguin

 c) an ice cream

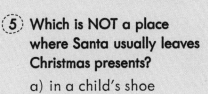

5 Which is NOT a place where Santa usually leaves Christmas presents?

a) in a child's shoe
b) in a stocking
c) in the oven

6 How old is an average Christmas tree?

a) 7 months
b) 7 years
c) 17 years

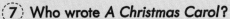

7 Who wrote *A Christmas Carol*?

a) Mark Twain
b) Lewis Carroll
c) Charles Dickens

8 A hundred years ago, what did people think Santa wore on his head instead of a hat?

a) a crown of mistletoe
b) a crown of holly
c) a crown of gold

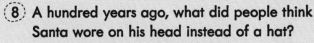

1. J.K. Rowling got married on Boxing Day, 2001. Which books is she famous for writing?
   a) *The Chronicles of Narnia*
   b) *The Moomins*
   c) *Harry Potter*

2. How do the residents of Gengenbach in Germany use their town as a giant Advent calendar?
   a) they make 24 chocolate "snowmen" and hide one somewhere in the town each day
   b) they decorate the 24 windows of the town hall and open one each day
   c) they hang lights on 24 trees in the town square and turn one on each day

3. Which are warmer:
   mittens or gloves?

4 In the Bible, which angel tells Mary she's going to have a baby?

a) Raphael   b) Michael   c) Gabriel

5 Model houses made from which food are popular Christmas decorations?

a) gingerbread
b) shortbread
c) toast

6 If Santa gave just one present to every child in the world, how many would he need?

a) 1.2 million
b) 2.2 billion
c) 4.2 trillion

1 Match Harry Potter's presents to the people who gave them during his first Christmas at Hogwarts.

a) a fifty pence piece   1. Albus Dumbledore

b) a wooden flute   2. the Dursleys

c) an invisibility cloak   3. Hagrid

2 According to the carol, what should you "deck the halls with" at Christmas?

a) treacle toffee

b) boughs of holly

c) something jolly

3 Which sauce is often eaten with turkey?

a) cranberry   b) redcurrant   c) strawberry

4 Which of these places is pronounced "Christmas" in the local language?

a) Kuala Lumpur   b) Kiritimati   c) Kidderminster

5 Along with the North Pole, where else do people think that Santa might live?

   a) Christmas Island
   b) Antarctica
   c) Lapland

6 What gifts did the Three Kings bring? Gold, frankincense and...

   a) ...myrrh
   b) ...sesame
   c) ...cinnamon

7 To be an official "white Christmas", how much snow must fall anywhere in the UK?

   a) 1ft (30cm)
   b) 1in (2.5cm)
   c) one snowflake

Match the five Christmas presents on this page with the decade they were first on sale. Then try the ones on the page opposite.

1) Slinky

2) Tamagotchi

3) Eating and wetting baby doll

4) Hula Hoop

5) Nintendo Wii

a) 1950s

b) 1990s

c) 1940s

d) 1970s

e) 2000s

1) Yo-yo

2) Elsa, Anna and Olaf cuddly dolls

3) Transformers

4) Etch A Sketch

5) Bubble wand

a) 2010s

b) 1920s

c) 1980s

d) 1930s

e) 1960s

1. **No two snowflakes are alike.**
   True or false?

2. **What's the main taste in a yule log dessert?**
   a) strawberry
   b) chocolate
   c) plum

3. **Which is a real American town?**
   a) Mince Pie
   b) Sugar Plum
   c) Santa Claus

4. **...And which is a real English place name?**
   a) Santa's Rump
   b) Jingle Bells
   c) Nut Crackers

5. **My eyes are two pieces of coal,**
   And my nose is a carrot.
   I like it when it's nice and cold.
   What am I?

6. **Instead of fir trees, what do people decorate in India?**
   a) banana trees
   b) baobab trees
   c) birch trees

7 If you open a window in an Advent calendar, what are you most likely to find?

  a) a coin
  b) a Christmas joke
  c) chocolate

8 What are frankincense and myrrh?

  a) tree resin
  b) food spice
  c) precious stones

9 Which muppets played Tiny Tim's parents in *A Muppet Christmas Carol*?

  a) Miss Piggy and Fozzie Bear
  b) Miss Piggy and Kermit the Frog
  c) Miss Piggy and Pepé the King Prawn

10 If the reindeer pulling Santa's sleigh have antlers, are they male or female?

11 During which war did British and German troops declare a day's truce on Christmas Day?

  a) The First World War
  b) The Second World War
  c) The Hundred Years' War

1) **How do you tell Santa what you want for Christmas?**
   a) write him a letter
   b) whisper into the chimney
   c) leave a list under your pillow

2) **Who kidnapped Santa Claus in the movie *The Nightmare Before Christmas*?**
   a) Johnny Pumpkinhead
   b) Jimmy Spindlefingers
   c) Jack Skellington

3) **Who's the legendary figure that spreads snow, frost and ice, and paints the leaves red and yellow?**
   a) Jill Chill
   b) Jack Frost
   c) The Ice Maiden

4) **What does the star on top of a Christmas tree represent?**
   a) Pole Star
   b) Star of Bethlehem
   c) the Sun

5) If you were on the Moon, what would be the easiest way of roasting a Christmas turkey?
   a) leave it outside in the daylight
   b) use rocket fuel to make a fire
   c) bury it underground

6) ...And if you wanted to freeze the leftovers after the meal, you could just leave them outside at night.
   True or false?

7) What's the highest selling Christmas single of all time?
   a) *Rudolph the Red-Nosed Reindeer*
   b) *All I Want for Christmas Is You*
   c) *White Christmas*

8) What do children in the Netherlands leave out instead of stockings?
   a) hats   b) gloves   c) shoes

9) According to the song, how many ships "came sailing in" on Christmas Day?
   a) two   b) three   c) four

Match the movies on this page to the year they were released on the page opposite.

1) The Polar Express

2) The Snowman

3) A Charlie Brown Christmas

4) Arthur Christmas

5) It's a Wonderful Life

6) Elf

7) The Grinch

8) The Nightmare before Christmas

9) Home Alone

10) The Muppet Christmas Carol

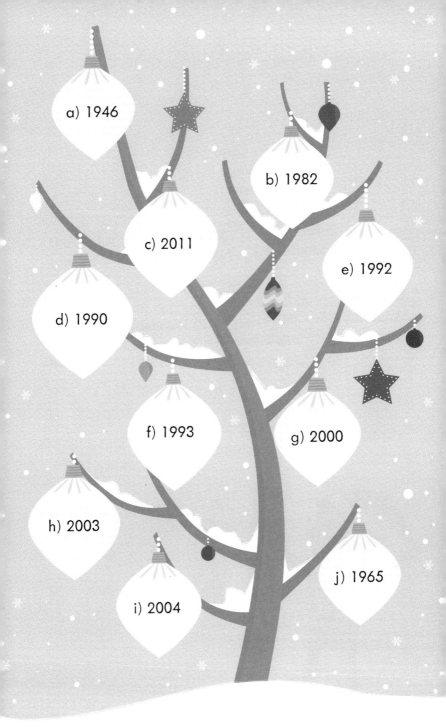

Match each song with the person or band who performed it.

1) Santa Claus Is Coming to Town

2) Last Christmas

3) Feliz Navidad

4) All I Want for Christmas Is You

5) Do They Know It's Christmas?

6) Rudolph the Red-Nosed Reindeer

7) Wonderful Christmastime

8) White Christmas

a) Bing Crosby

b) José Feliciano

c) Gene Autry

d) Paul McCartney

e) The Jackson 5

f) Mariah Carey

g) Wham!

h) Band Aid

1. In 1968, the crew of Apollo 8 became the first astronauts to celebrate Christmas in space. What else were they first to do?
   a) the first humans to land on Mars
   b) the first humans to orbit the Moon
   c) the first humans to encounter aliens

2. When are the Twelve Days of Christmas?
   a) December 1st – December 12th
   b) December 14th – December 25th
   c) December 25th – January 5th

3. The first successful trial of which world-changing invention took place on Christmas Day 1990?
   a) the World Wide Web
   b) the telephone
   c) the hoverboard

4. Which is NOT a traditional use of bells on sleighs?
   a) warning people to get out of the way
   b) warding off evil spirits
   c) keeping the horses awake

18

1 Which marmalade-loving bear has two birthdays, one on Christmas Day and one on the 25th of June?

a) Paddington   b) Winnie-the-Pooh   c) Baloo

2 Which of Santa's reindeer shares a name with a Roman god of love?

a) Vixen   b) Cupid   c) Prancer

3 In the Nativity story, an angel announces the birth of Jesus to people working at night near Bethlehem. Who are they?

a) guards   b) thieves   c) shepherds

4 No one's sure whether I live at the North Pole or in Lapland – it's a secret!
When I laugh my round belly shakes like a bowlful of jelly.

Who am I?

5 Why did Mary and Joseph travel to Egypt after Jesus's birth?
   a) they wanted to see the pyramids
   b) they were captured by slave traders
   c) King Herod wanted to kill Jesus

6 In Britain, which sweet treat is often soaked in brandy and set on fire?
   a) Christmas pudding
   b) gingerbread men
   c) yule log

7 Which is NOT a common type of Christmas tree?
   a) Noble fir
   b) Norway spruce
   c) Prickly pear cactus

8 The blades on ice skates were originally made from:
   a) wood
   b) bone
   c) plastic

1 Traditionally, children in Italy are given gifts on Twelfth Night by Befana. Who is Befana?

a) a fairy　　b) a witch　　c) a goblin

2 According to the poem beginning "Twas the night before Christmas", what happens when Santa laughs?

a) he ho ho hos from his head to his toes
b) Rudolph's nose shines bright
c) his belly shakes like a bowl full of jelly

3 The biggest Christmas stocking ever made was over 51m (167ft) tall and over 21m (69ft) wide. What presents were put inside?

a) watermelons
b) balloons filled with sweets
c) none – it held a giant papier-mâché foot

4 I plodded from Nazareth to Bethlehem with Mary and Joseph.
They stayed with me in a stable.

Who am I?

5 Which Christmas carol mentions the stars in the night sky?

a) *Away in a Manger*
b) *The Holly and the Ivy*
c) *The Twelve Days of Christmas*

6 Where would you NOT hang a stocking for Santa?

a) from the mantelpiece
b) at the end of your bed
c) in the bathroom

7 Which type of plant is often eaten with Christmas dinner?

a) Rotterdam turnip
b) Brussels sprout
c) Helsinki carrot

8 During The Second World War, some people stopped making Advent calendars. Why?

a) to save paper
b) to save chocolate
c) Christmas wasn't celebrated

9 Is a snowflake round like a ball or flat like a pancake?

Using the words from the song *The Twelve Days of Christmas*, match each day to the right gift.

2) Second day

3) Third day

4) Fourth day

1) First day

5) Fifth day

6) Sixth day

9) Ninth day

8) Eighth day

7) Seventh day

10) Tenth day

11) Eleventh day

12) Twelfth day

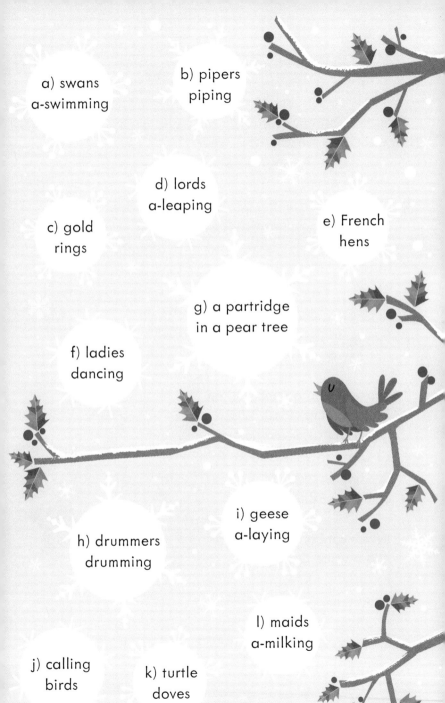

a) swans a-swimming

b) pipers piping

c) gold rings

d) lords a-leaping

e) French hens

f) ladies dancing

g) a partridge in a pear tree

h) drummers drumming

i) geese a-laying

j) calling birds

k) turtle doves

l) maids a-milking

(1) In the Christmas carol *The Holly and the Ivy*, what does the holly tree wear?

a) a gown   b) a crown   c) a frown

(2) Postal workers in the UK used to wear bright red uniforms. What was their nickname?

a) sparrows   b) robins   c) pigeons

(3) Johnny Depp got married on Christmas Eve, 1983. Which movie character did he play?

a) Captain Jack Sparrow
b) Luke Skywalker
c) James Bond

(4) Which capital city has never had a white Christmas?

a) Oslo in Norway
b) Athens, Greece
c) Jakarta, Indonesia

5. I was a mean, grasping old man...
...and Scrooge's ex-business partner.
I appeared in his door-knocker and scared
him half to death.
Who am I?

6. Which of these reindeer facts isn't true?
a) they live at the North Pole
b) they can see ultraviolet light
c) their eyes are golden in summer and blue in winter

7. What guided the Three Kings to Bethlehem?
a) a star   b) a map   c) a blind prophet

8. Would Santa be warmer or colder if he lived
at the South Pole?

9. If you're vegetarian, what might
you eat instead of meat for
Christmas dinner?
a) pine roast
b) pot roast
c) nut roast

In what order do these events happen
in the story of Jesus's birth?

(a) The shepherds go to Bethlehem and find Jesus
wrapped up warm and lying in a manger.

(b) Mary and Joseph are turned away from
the inn because all the beds are taken.

(c) The angel Gabriel visits Mary in Nazareth
and tells her she'll give birth to a child.

(d) Mary and Joseph escape Bethlehem under cover of
darkness. They head for Egypt, where they'll be safe.

(e) During the night, Mary gives birth to a
baby boy, and names him Jesus.

(f) Mary and Joseph find an empty stable,
and decide to spend the night there.

(g) After they leave, an angel warns
Joseph that King Herod is searching
for Jesus, and wants to kill him.

(h) Mary and Joseph set off for Bethlehem, because
Joseph needs to register there for a census.

(i) They offer gifts of gold, frankincense and myrrh.

(j) A few years later, Herod dies, so
Mary and Joseph return to Nazareth.

(k) Some time later, three wise men arrive. They've
journeyed a long way and were guided by a star.

(l) Out in the fields, shepherds are visited by
an angel who announces Jesus's birth.

1 Which *Harry Potter* character could wear Christmas stockings as if they were normal-sized socks?

a) Severus Snape
b) Lord Voldemort
c) Hagrid

2 Mince pies contain meat.

True or false?

3 What are Christmas cakes traditionally covered in?

a) marzipan and icing
b) strawberries and cream
c) chocolate and sprinkles

4 Which is NOT a Christmas song in New Zealand?

a) *Sticky Beak the Kiwi*
b) *A Pukeko in a Ponga Tree*
c) *We Three Blokes of Wellington Are*

5 How many windows are there in an Advent calendar?

a) 12   b) 24   c) 25

6 Which Christmas cards are more popular:

paper cards or e-cards?

7 I was born on Christmas Day in 1642. I explained how gravity works and light shines. Who am I?

a) Isaac Newton
b) Albert Einstein
c) Stephen Hawking

(1) **The biggest ever snowman was as tall as how many giraffes standing one on top of the other?**

a) 2 giraffes   b) 7 giraffes   c) 13 giraffes

(2) **In South America, children leave shoes under their beds for the Three Kings to fill with gifts. What do they leave for the camels?**

a) potatoes   b) carrots   c) straw

(3) **How many reindeer pull Santa's sleigh (including Rudolph)?**

a) 7   b) 8   c) 9

(4) **In the song *Santa Claus Is Coming to Town*, why does Santa keep a list?**

a) to tell if you've been naughty or nice
b) so he doesn't visit anyone twice
c) to record every present's price

5 Where would you find a Christmas tree growing in the wild?

   a) Russia
   b) Egypt
   c) Antarctica

6 In Norway, it's said that witches come out on Christmas Eve. How do people prepare for this?

   a) keep their cauldrons full of chicken soup
   b) hide their broomsticks before bed
   c) avoid black cats all day

7 Where is it always a white Christmas in the United States?

   a) San Francisco, California
   b) Fort Worth, Texas
   c) Fairbanks, Alaska

8 If Santa lives at the North Pole all year round, how often does he see the Sun rise?

   a) once   b) 52 times   c) 365 times

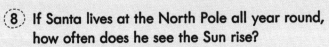

1. **Complete the movie title: *It's a Wonderful...*?**
   a) Day for Opening Presents
   b) Time of the Year
   c) Life

2. **Which member of The Beatles was given his first drum kit on Christmas Day 1959?**
   a) Ringo Starr
   b) John Lennon
   c) Paul McCartney

3. **Which animal is best at walking on ice?**
   a) moose   b) reindeer   c) buffalo

4. **What are the elves who work for Santa called?**
   a) Santa's green collar workers
   b) Santa's secret service
   c) Santa's little helpers

5. **If you're scared of snowflakes, you have:**
   a) claustrophobia
   b) arachnophobia
   c) chionophobia

6. **Who were the first to visit Jesus in the stable?**
   a) the Three Kings   b) shepherds   c) soldiers

7. **One day after Christmas, I looked down from my castle and saw a poor man gathering winter fuel. I am the king of Bohemia.**
   Who am I?

8. **Which series of books was written by Stephenie Meyer, born on Christmas Eve 1973?**
   a) *Twilight*
   b) *His Dark Materials*
   c) *The Hunger Games*

9. **When were trees first brought indoors and decorated for Christmas?**
   a) 1200
   b) 1700
   c) 2000

1. **When was the first Christmas card printed?**
   a) 1043   b) 1843   c) 2003

2. **At Christmas in Britain, people eat sugary treats in the shape of a...**
   a) lion   b) mouse   c) elephant

3. **Put me at the foot of your bed on Christmas Eve, and you might find some gifts inside me next day.**
   What am I?

4. **"Oh the weather outside is frightful, But the fire is so delightful..." These are the opening lines to which song?**
   a) *Let it Snow! Let it Snow! Let it Snow!*
   b) *Have Yourself a Merry Little Christmas*
   c) *Frosty the Snowman*

5. **At Christmastime in the Alps, it's said the Krampus comes out to scare naughty children. What does he look like?**
   a) he has a toad's body and a forked tongue
   b) he has a dragon's wings and fish gills
   c) he has goat's hooves and long horns

6 I was the ruler of Judea.
I heard "The King of the Jews" was born in Bethlehem.
That sounded like trouble – I'm the King of the Jews!
So I tried to have him killed.

Who am I?

7 In a Christmas ballet called *The Nutcracker*,
what does the nutcracker turn into?

a) a prince
b) a witch
c) Grandfather Frost

8 The nuts of which tree are roasted over an
open fire at Christmas?

a) sweet chestnut
b) coconut
c) oak

9 Which TV family has a pet dog
named Santa's Little Helper?

a) the Addams Family
b) the Flintstones
c) the Simpsons

10 Christmas trees drop their
leaves in summer.

True or false?

Around the world, people say "Merry Christmas" in different ways. Match the six phrases on this page to the correct language, then try the ones on the page opposite.

1) Joyeux Noël

2) عيد ا ميلاد ا سعيد
(eid al milad al saeed)

3) God Jul

4) 圣诞节快乐
(shèngdàn jié kuàilè)

5) Krismasi Njema

6) Feliz Navidad

a) Norwegian

b) Spanish

c) Chinese

d) Swahili

e) Arabic

f) French

1) Fröhliche Weihnachten

2) メリークリスマス
(merikurisumasu)

3) Feliz Natal

4) क्रिसमस की बधाई
(krisamas kee badhaee)

5) Счастливого Рождества
(schastlivovo rozhdestva)

6) Buon Natale

a) Russian

b) German

c) Japanese

d) Italian

e) Portuguese

f) Hindi

1 Which sci-fi hero saved his home planet of Gallifrey in a town called Christmas?

a) Luke Skywalker
b) Doctor Who
c) Spock

2 Which Christian saint is known for giving out presents like Santa Claus?

a) St. Nicholas   b) St. John   c) St. Stephen

3 Adelaide holds the record for Australia's hottest ever Christmas. How hot was it?

a) 32.1°C (89.8°F)
b) 42.1°C (107.8°F)
c) 52.1°C (125.8°F)

4 Dormice are deep in a long winter sleep at Christmas. What's this called?

a) meditation
b) hibernation
c) evaporation

5 Reindeer antlers are made from the same material as your:

a) teeth   b) nails   c) bones

6 Which character in traditional Nativity plays does not actually appear in the Bible's account of the Nativity?

a) the donkey

b) the innkeeper

c) the angel Gabriel

7 Which Disney film was released on Christmas Day 1963?

a) *Frozen*

b) *Monsters Inc.*

c) *The Sword in the Stone*

8 In Iceland at Christmas, thirteen mischievous Yule Lads leave gifts for good children... and what for naughty children?

a) a list of chores

b) a smelly fish

c) a rotting potato

1 **Which of these is a real thing celebrated in Britain in December?**
a) Christmas Jumper (Sweater) Day
b) Woolly Hat Day
c) Warm Socks Day

2 **I grew in a forest,
and my jacket is leathery and brown.
I was roasted over an open fire.**
What am I?

3 **Druids in Ancient Britain used a golden sickle to cut the berries from which traditional Christmas plant?**
a) holly   b) mistletoe   c) elderflower

4 **Which treats are often hung from Christmas trees?**
a) mince pies   b) meatballs   c) candy canes

5 **Where does the Grinch who stole Christmas live?**
a) Jungle of Nool   b) Mount Crumpit   c) Whoville

6 Who's the main character in the story called *A Christmas Carol*?

a) Edwin Scrooge

b) Edward Scrooge

c) Ebenezer Scrooge

7 Which country plays a cricket test match every Boxing Day?

a) Australia   b) Sri Lanka   c) Pakistan

8 During the Christmas truce between British and German soldiers in The First World War, which carol did the soldiers sing together?

a) *O Little Town of Bethlehem*

b) *Silent Night*

c) *O Christmas Tree*

9 Which animal would Santa never see near the North Pole?

a) penguin   b) polar bear   c) seal

10 Where's Santa Claus called Joulupukki, which means "Christmas goat"?

a) Australia

b) India

c) Finland

Match the words with the song they're from.

1) "And the bells are ringing out for Christmas Day"

2) "Earth stood hard as iron, water like a stone"

3) "The people far below are sleeping as we fly"

4) "Your brain is full of spiders, you have garlic in your soul"

5) "All is calm, all is bright"

a) *You're a mean one, Mr. Grinch*

b) *Silent Night*

c) *In the Bleak Midwinter*

d) *Walking in the Air*

e) *Fairytale of New York*

1. **Where are you most likely to have your Christmas food cooked on a barbecue grill?**
   a) Australia
   b) Finland
   c) Canada

2. **What's the most popular decoration to put on top of a Christmas tree?**
   a) a bell   b) a star   c) an angel

3. **What name does Santa Claus give for himself in the movie *Miracle on 34th Street*?**
   a) Nicholas Saint
   b) Kris Kringle
   c) Noel Christmas

4. **How many turkeys are eaten around the world each Christmas?**
   a) 22,000
   b) 220,000
   c) 22,000,000

Complete these Christmas jokes by matching the questions with their punchlines.

1) What carol does a dog like best?

2) What goes red white, red white, red white?

3) How does Santa keep his head warm?

4) What do you get when you cross a snowman with a vampire?

5) What do you sing at a snowman's birthday party?

6) Why was the snowman looking through the carrots?

7) What did Adam say to his wife on the day before Christmas?

8) Where does Santa stay when he's on vacation?

9) How does Good King Wenceslas like his pizzas?

10) What do you get if you eat Christmas decorations?

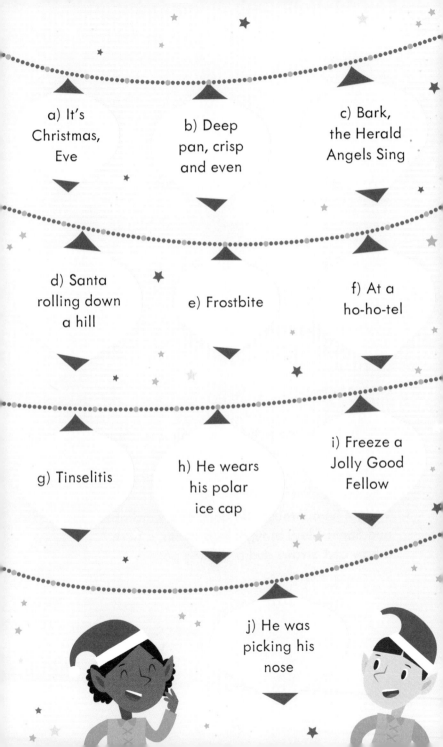

a) It's Christmas, Eve

b) Deep pan, crisp and even

c) Bark, the Herald Angels Sing

d) Santa rolling down a hill

e) Frostbite

f) At a ho-ho-tel

g) Tinselitis

h) He wears his polar ice cap

i) Freeze a Jolly Good Fellow

j) He was picking his nose

1 If someone is described as a "scrooge," what are they?

a) overweight   b) miserly   c) stubborn

2 What's a baby reindeer called?

a) deerlet   b) pup   c) calf

3 Does mistletoe have:

a) white berries?
b) black berries?
c) red berries?

4 Which British monarch fell through their chair while delivering their Christmas speech in 1932?

a) Victoria   b) George V   c) Elizabeth II

5 We got here through the back of a wardrobe, and Santa Claus brought us a sword, a horn, a bow and arrows and a healing potion.

Where are we?

Answers

① **1.** c **2.** c **3.** b **4.** a **5.** a **6.** b **7.** false **8.** b (During the Earth's orbit, when the Northern Hemisphere is tilted away from the Sun, the Southern Hemisphere is tilted towards it.) **9.** a

② **1.** b **2.** c **3.** c **4.** b **5.** a **6.** b **7.** a **8.** a

③ **1.** b **2.** c **3.** b **4.** false **5.** a **6.** c **7.** a **8.** Rudolph the red-nosed reindeer **9.** b

④ **1.** a (If you head in the direction of the North Star, you'll be going north.) **2.** c **3.** a **4.** b **5.** b **6.** a Christmas tree **7.** c **8.** a

⑤ **1.** c **2.** b (Oliver Cromwell was a leader of the Parliamentarians during the English Civil War. They fought King Charles I and his supporters for control of the country. When the Parliamentarians won, they banned Christmas. At the time, Christmas celebrations lasted twelve days, and many people thought they were too extravagant. Christmas was also seen as a Catholic celebration, and Catholicism was a religion outlawed in England. The ban on Christmas was lifted in 1660, when the Parliamentarians were forced out by King Charles II and his supporters.) **3.** a (Often there's a fifth candle lit on Christmas Eve or Christmas Day.) **4.** b **5.** a **6.** false **7.** c

⑥ **1.** d **2.** g **3.** h **4.** b **5.** f **6.** a **7.** i **8.** c **9.** e

⑦ **1.** b **2.** the Grinch **3.** a **4.** b **5.** a **6.** a **7.** c **8.** true (Ice is lighter than water.)

⑧ **1.** c **2.** b **3.** a **4.** a **5.** c **6.** b **7.** c **8.** b

9 **1.** c **2.** b **3.** mittens (Mittens have less surface area in contact with the cold air, and also keep your warm fingers in contact with each other.) **4.** c **5.** a **6.** b

10 **1.** a2, b3, c1 **2.** b **3.** a **4.** b **5.** c (Lapland is a region that stretches across the northern parts of Norway, Sweden and Finland, as well as part of north-western Russia.) **6.** a **7.** c

11 1c, **2**b, **3**d, **4**a, **5**e

12 1b, **2**a, **3**c, **4**e, **5**d

13 **1.** true (Although occasionally tiny snow crystals fall fom the sky. These haven't yet grown into snowflakes, and look very similar to each other.) **2.** b **3.** c **4.** c (Nut Crackers is the name of a huge boulder on a hill in Devon, England.) **5.** a snowman **6.** a **7.** c **8.** a (They were used as perfume and incense, and myrrh was also used in medicine.) **9.** b **10.** female (By mid-December, male reindeer have shed their antlers.) **11.** a

14 **1.** a **2.** c **3.** b **4.** b (In the Nativity story, the Star of Bethlehem guided the Three Kings to the place where Jesus was born.) **5.** a (The temperature on the Moon hits 123°C (253°F) during the day.) **6.** true (The temperature on the Moon drops to -173°C (-279°F) at night.) **7.** c **8.** c **9.** b

15 1i, **2**b, **3**j, **4**c, **5**a, **6**h, **7**g, **8**f, **9**d, **10**e

16 1e, **2**g, **3**b, **4**f, **5**h, **6**c, **7**d, **8**a

17 **1.** b **2.** c **3.** a **4.** c

18 1. a 2. b 3. c 4. Santa Claus 5. c (King Herod had heard that people were calling Jesus the "King of the Jews". Herod had been named King of the Jews by the Romans, so he wanted to crush any threat to his throne.) 6. a 7. c 8. b

19 1. b 2. c 3. b 4. a donkey 5. a 6. c 7. b 8. a 9. flat

20 1g, 2k, 3e, 4j, 5c, 6i, 7a, 8l, 9f, 10d, 11b, 12h

21 1. b 2. b 3. a 4. c 5. Jacob Marley 6. a (Reindeer mainly eat plants and lichen, and these don't grow at the North Pole because there's no soil, only ice.) 7. a 8. colder (The South Pole is in Antarctica, which is the highest continent in the world because it's covered by a sheet of ice so thick it swallows up mountains.) 9. c

22 c, h, b, f, e, l, a, k, i, g, d, j

23 1. c 2. false (Mince pies contain something called mincemeat, but this type of mincemeat doesn't contain meat. It did in the past, but now it's just made from dried fruit and spices.) 3. a 4. c 5. b 6. paper cards 7. a

24 1. b (It was 37m (122ft) tall and took one month to build.) 2. c 3. c 4. a 5. a 6. b 7. c 8. a (For half the year the North Pole is tilted permanently away from the Sun, and for the other half it's tilted permanently towards it.)

25 1. c 2. a 3. b (Their hooves have hard rims that dig into the ice.) 4. c 5. c 6. b 7. King Wenceslas 8. a 9. b

26 1. b 2. b 3. a stocking 4. a 5. c 6. King Herod 7. a 8. a 9. c 10. false (Most Christmas trees are spruce, pine or fir trees – which are all evergreen.)

27 1f, 2e, 3a, 4c, 5d, 6b

28 1b, 2c, 3e, 4f, 5a, 6d

29 1. b 2. a 3. b 4. b 5. c 6. a 7. c 8. c

30 1. a 2. a chestnut 3. b 4. c 5. b 6. c 7. a 8. b 9. a (Penguins don't live at the North Pole.) 10. c

31 1e, 2c, 3d, 4a, 5b

32 1. a 2. b 3. b 4. c

33 1c, 2d, 3h, 4e, 5i, 6j, 7a, 8f, 9b, 10g

34 1. b 2. c 3. a 4. b 5. Narnia

Cover questions

Are any two snowflakes alike? No
Do female reindeer have antlers? Yes
Who helps Santa in his workshop? Elves

Edited by Simon Tudhope
Designed and illustrated by Kate Rimmer

With thanks to Alex Frith, Jerome Martin,
Minna Lacey, Lucy Bowman and James Maclaine

First published in 2016 by Usborne Publishing Ltd, 83–85 Saffron Hill, London ECIN 8RT, England.
Copyright © 2016 Usborne Publishing Ltd. The name Usborne and the devices ♀♛are Trade Marks of Usborne Publishing Ltd.
All rights reserved. No part of this publication may be reproduced, stored in a retrieval system, or transmitted in any form or
by any means, electronic, mechanical, photocopying, recording or otherwise, without the prior permission of the publisher.
UE. This edition first published in America 2016. Printed in the UAE.